What Are Drugs?

A Drug-Free Kids Book

Gretchen Super
Illustrated by Blanche Sims

TWENTY-FIRST CENTURY BOOKS
FREDERICK, MARYLAND

Published by
Twenty-First Century Books
38 South Market Street
Frederick, Maryland 21701

Text Copyright © 1990
Twenty-First Century Books

Illustrations Copyright © 1990
Blanche Sims

Printed in the United States of America

10 9 8 7 6 5 4 3 2

Library of Congress Cataloging in Publication Data

Super, Gretchen
What Are Drugs?
Illustrated by Blanche Sims

(A Drug-Free Kids Book)
Includes bibliographical references.
Summary: Examines, in simple text and illustrations,
what drugs are, what they can do to your body,
and the problems of drug addiction.
1. Drug abuse—Juvenile literature.
2. Drugs—Juvenile literature.
[1. Drugs. 2. Drug abuse.]
I. Sims, Blanche, ill. II. Title.
III. Series: Drug-Free Kids.
HV5801.S838   1990
362.29—dc20   90-31120 CIP AC
ISBN 0-941477-87-8

Table of Contents

Chapter 1

This Is Your Book

This is a book about drugs.

You hear about drugs a lot.
You hear about them at home.
You hear about them at school.

What do you hear about drugs?

You hear that drugs can hurt you.
You hear that you should say "No"
to drugs.

But do you know what drugs are?
Do you know what they look like?
Do you know why they can hurt you?

Drugs change the way the body works.
They change the way the brain works.

Drugs change the way people think.
They change the way people feel.
They change the way people act.

There are many kinds of drugs.
Some drugs are helpful.
They are used as medicine.
Some drugs are harmful.
And even medicines can be harmful
if they are not used in the right way.

This book will show you what drugs
are and what they do.
And it will help you to say "No"
to drugs.

Saying "No" to drugs is a big job.
But there are people to help you.
And you can help get the job done, too.

Chapter 2

This Is Your Body

Look at your body.
It has many parts.
There are parts on the outside.
There are parts on the inside.

You can see the outside parts.
Your body has arms and legs.
It has eyes and ears.
It has a nose and a mouth.
It has lots of skin.

You cannot see the inside parts.
You can't see the stomach.
You can't see the lungs or the bones.
You can't see the heart or the brain.

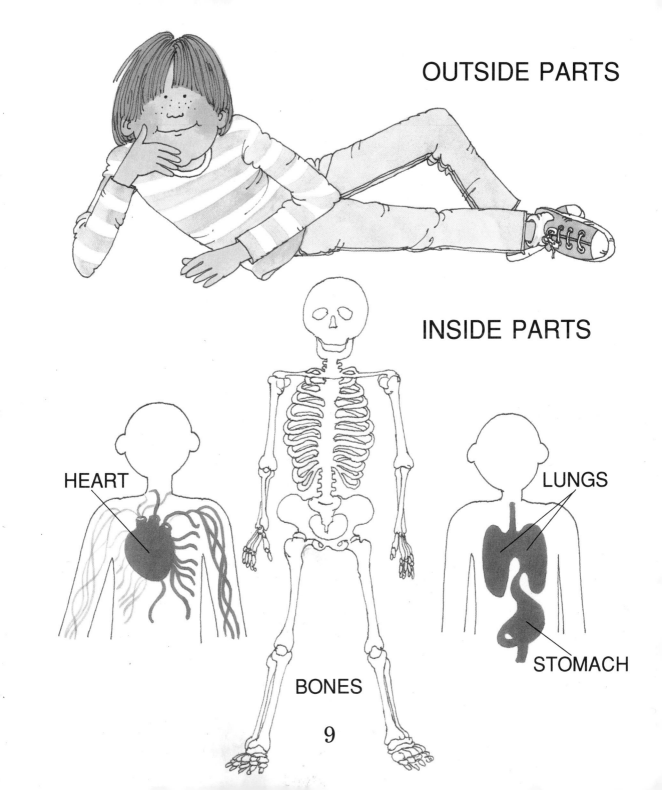

OUTSIDE PARTS

INSIDE PARTS

HEART

LUNGS

STOMACH

BONES

9

Your body can do wonderful things.
The outside parts of your body tell
you about the world.
And they help you move around in
the world.

Your eyes let you see.
Your ears let you hear.
Your nose lets you smell.
Your mouth lets you taste.
Your skin lets you touch.

Your legs let you walk and run.
They let you jump as high as you can.
Your arms let you throw and wave.
They let you stand on your hands.

What do the inside parts
of your body do?
They keep you alive and healthy.
Your lungs breathe in and out.
Your heart pumps blood
to every part of your body.
Your stomach uses the food you eat
to help you grow.
Your bones hold your body together.

And what about your brain?
Your brain is in charge of your body.

Your brain tells your body what to do.
It tells your eyes what they see.
It tells your arms and legs
how to move.
It tells your lungs and heart
how to work.

Your brain is also in charge
of your thoughts.
It lets you think and dream.

Your brain is in charge
of your feelings, too.
It makes you happy or sad.

13

Your body is wonderful,
inside and outside.
And it can do wonderful things.

But it cannot do them by itself.
It needs help from you.
You have to keep your body healthy.

Chapter 3

It's Your Health

"My body needs help from me?"
you may ask.
"How can I help my body?"

You help your body in many ways.
You help your body when you get
a good night's sleep.
That helps your body get the rest
it needs.

You help your body when you swim
or hike or play outdoor games.
That helps your body get strong.

You help your body when you eat
healthy foods.
Most of the things you eat or drink
are good for your body.
Your body needs healthy foods to
grow and be strong.

But sometimes your body gets sick.
You know what it is like to be sick.
Maybe you have to stay home
from school.
Maybe you have to go to the doctor.

Sometimes the doctor gives you
medicine to make you feel better.
The doctor tells you what kind
of medicine to take.
The doctor tells you how much
medicine to take.
The doctor tells you when
to take it.

Your parents go to the store
to buy your medicine.
Your parents give you the medicine
just the way the doctor says.

Soon you start to feel better.
The medicine is working.
You help your body when you take
your medicine.

There are many ways you help
your body.
But you can also hurt your body.

Some things you put in your body
are not helpful.
There are foods and drinks that do
not help your body.

There are some things
that hurt your body.
You learned about poisons
when you were younger.
You learned that poisons
will hurt your body.

Some drugs are like poison.
They hurt the body.

Some drugs change the body when it
does not need to be changed.
They make people sick.

Even medicine can make you sick.
Medicine can hurt you if you take it
in the wrong way.
It is never safe for you to take
medicine by yourself.

Keeping your body healthy
is a big job.
But there are people to help you.
And you can help get the job done, too.

Chapter 4

Drugs You Should Know About

There are many different drugs.
You should know about some of these
drugs.

Alcohol

Alcohol is a drug found in drinks
like beer and wine.

You may have seen people
drinking alcohol.
Your Mom and Dad may drink beer
with dinner.
They may have a glass of wine
with their friends.
It is not against the law
for grown-up people to drink alcohol.

But alcohol can be harmful.
It makes it hard for the outside
parts of the body to work.
It makes it hard to see well and
to speak clearly.
It can make it hard to walk
and even to stand up.

Alcohol can hurt the inside parts
of the body, too.
It can make people sick.
Alcohol can also hurt the brain.
It changes the way people think.
It changes the way people feel.
They may get confused or sad or angry.

It is never safe for kids to use alcohol.
It is always against the law for kids
to use alcohol.

Nicotine

Nicotine is a drug found in things
made from the tobacco plant.
Cigarettes and cigars are made
from tobacco.
So are pipe and chewing tobacco.

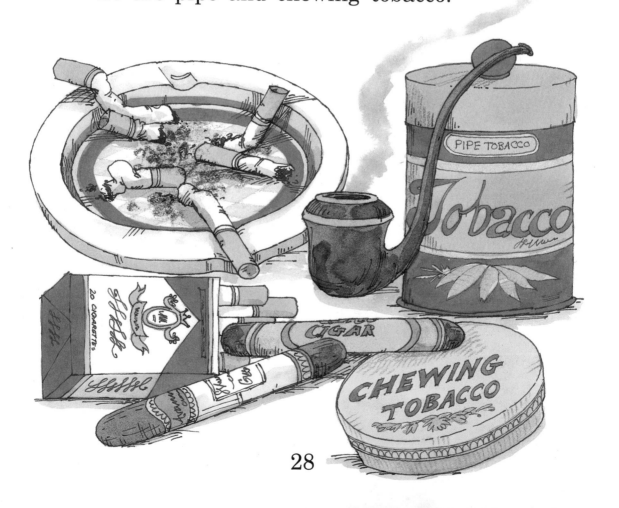

28

Tobacco hurts the people who use it.
People who smoke tobacco get sick
more than other people.

Tobacco smoke hurts the lungs.
It makes it hard for the lungs
to breathe.
Tobacco smoke hurts the heart.
It makes it hard for the heart
to pump blood.

Tobacco causes a disease called cancer.
Cancer kills many people every year.

It is not against the law
for grown-up people to use nicotine.
But it is not safe for them to use it.
And tobacco is very dangerous
for kids to use.

Marijuana

Marijuana comes from a plant, too.
It comes from the cannabis plant.
It looks like shredded leaves.
Another name for marijuana is pot.

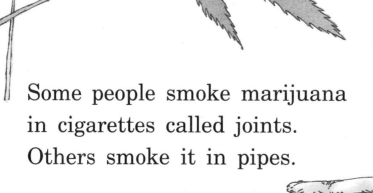

Some people smoke marijuana
in cigarettes called joints.
Others smoke it in pipes.

Like alcohol and tobacco, marijuana
hurts the people who use it.
It is a dangerous drug.

Marijuana changes the way
the body works.
It hurts the lungs and heart.
It causes cancer, too.

Marijuana changes the way
the brain works.
It makes it hard to think clearly.
It makes it hard to learn and
remember things.

It is against the law for grown-up
people to use marijuana.
It is against the law for everyone
to use marijuana.

Cocaine and Crack

Cocaine comes from the coca plant.
It is a white, powdery drug.
It looks like powdered sugar.
But cocaine is not like
powdered sugar.
Cocaine is a very dangerous drug.

Some people sniff the cocaine powder
up their noses.
Some people smoke cocaine in pipes.
They smoke little bits of cocaine
called crack.
Other people give themselves shots
of cocaine with needles.

Like other drugs, cocaine hurts
the body and the brain.
It hurts the heart.
It hurts the lungs.
And it is very hard for people to stop
using cocaine once they start.
Cocaine can even kill people who use it.

Like marijuana, it is against the law
for everyone to use cocaine.

Chapter 5

Why People Use Drugs

Why do people use drugs?

Some people do not know the facts
about drugs.
They think drugs are safe.
Some people think they will not
be hurt by drugs.
They think drugs only hurt other people.

What are the facts about drugs?

The fact is that drugs
are not safe to use.
The fact is that drugs
make people sick.

People start to use drugs
for many reasons.

They think it will be fun.
They think it will make them happy.
They think it will be a way
to make friends.

The fact is that using drugs gets
people in trouble.

The fact is that drugs do not make people happy.

The fact is that using drugs is no way to make friends.

There is one more reason
why people use drugs.
Some people use drugs because
they feel that they must have drugs.
They are addicted to drugs.
People who are addicted to drugs
feel sick if they do not use drugs.

It is very hard for people who are
addicted to drugs to stop using them.
People who are addicted to drugs
need special help to stop using drugs.

The best way to stop using drugs
is not to start.
The best way to stop drug problems
is to be a drug-free kid.
A drug-free kid never uses drugs.

Chapter 6

Be a Drug-Free Kid

You know that drugs hurt people.
You know that they will hurt you
if you use them.
You want to say "No" to drugs.

You want a healthy body.
You want to be happy.
You want to be smart.
You want to be a drug-free kid.

Here are some ideas to keep you safe:

- If someone offers you drugs, say "No." Walk away.

- If you know kids who use drugs, stay away from them.

- If you find drugs, don't pick them up.
Never pick up matches, or needles, or
anything else people use to take drugs.

If any of these things happens
to you, go get help.

Who should you go to for help?
What should you do if you have more
questions about drugs?

Find a grown-up to talk to.
Find a grown-up you like and trust.

Ask them your questions.
Tell them what is on your mind.

It could be your Mom
or Dad.
It could be your teacher.
It could be your doctor.

Remember that there are people
who love and care about you.
There are people who want you
to live a happy and healthy life.
There are always people who will
listen to you.
There are always people who will
help you to be a drug-free kid.

44

Being a drug-free kid is a big job.
But there are people to help you.
And you can help get the job done, too.

You can do it!

Words You Need to Know

Being a drug-free kid is a big job. But you can do it. Knowing about drugs will help you stay drug-free. Here are some words you need to know.

addicted   when someone can't stop using drugs

alcohol   a drug found in drinks like beer and wine

cocaine   a drug that comes from the coca plant

crack   a kind of cocaine that is smoked

drug   something that changes the way the body and brain work

joint   a marijuana cigarette

marijuana   a drug that comes from the cannabis plant

medicine   the kind of drug a doctor gives you when you are sick

nicotine   a drug found in things made from the tobacco plant

peer pressure   when other people make you feel that you have to do something

poison   something that hurts the body if you eat or drink it

Index

Drugs and Our Children

A Note to Parents, Teachers, and Librarians

Drug-Free Kids is a book series for children ages 5 to 8. Our children, even at this early age, hear about drugs, but they may not understand what the drug problem is about. They know that drugs are a problem. But they may not know why or how.

This series was written to help young children understand why and how drugs are a problem. Drug-Free Kids places the problem of drug use within a framework of issues children may already know about—issues such as health and wellness, social responsibility, and personal choice. The need to say "No" to drugs is presented not as a question separate from the other important decisions our children have to face, but as one part of an outlook on life that enables them to grow up happy and healthy.

These books are designed to encourage independent reading. But no book series on drugs can take the place of active adult involvement in the lives of our children. I hope you will take the time to read these books with your children or students. They will have questions, and you may not have all the answers. But Drug-Free Kids gives us an excellent start. It opens a dialogue on one of the most important challenges of our time: how to teach our children to say "No" to drugs.

Lee Dogoloff, Executive Director
American Council for Drug Education